Sparrow

Belinda Broughton

Sparrow

Poems of a Refugee

Acknowledgements

Thanks to Graham Rowlands, Kate Deller-Evans, Margaret Wilson,
Ida Maglai, my wonderful secondary-school teacher Jessie Landsberg
(who could see past atrocious spelling and handwriting),
and my poet friends from First Draft, Hills Poets
and Friendly Street Poets.

Dedication

I wish to thank my three children, Dirk Janek, Miklos Janek,
and Hana Edwards, to whom this book is dedicated.
May your children's children enjoy it.

And finally and especially, thanks to Ervin Janek:
my heart, my love, my husband and my protagonist!

Sparrow: Poems of a Refugee
ISBN 978 1 74027 989 5
Copyright © text Belinda Broughton 2015

First published 2015 by
GINNINDERRA PRESS
PO Box 3461 Port Adelaide SA 5015
www.ginninderrapress.com.au

Contents

Sparrow	9
Conception	11
Going to Market	12
Zsuzsi	13
Mud Cake	14
The First Lie	15
René	16
The Cross	17
Snow	18
Going to the Hitler Youth	19
A Shiny Stone	20
The Train	21
Budapest Hospital	22
Orion's Belt	23
Grandfather	24
The Washroom	25
Meat	26
Taking Advantage of the Situation	27
Grandmother	28
Of God and Oxen	29
Girls	30
The Doctor	31
The Birthday Poem	32
Sparrow	34
Dawn on Lake Balaton	35
Not Murder	36
Árpád	37
Deer in the Woods	39
Comrade Várodi	41
Doves	43
Boots	45
Bored Keepers	46

Happiness	47
The Opening of the Jail	48
On Lenin Körút, Budapest, 1956	49
Old Mrs Szabo	51
The National Guard	52
The White Coat	53
Peer Pressure	54
Why to Not be Rude to Soldiers	56
A Little Outing	57
Running for the Border	58
When I came to the River Zala	59
The Old Woman	60
2 December 1956, Hungarian Border	61
My First Shave	62
Speaking German	63
Eating with Knives	64
The Monastery	65
Sport-heart	67
Baroness Eliza Mernhoff and Her Horse	69
Doves	70
Decisions	71
Kookaburra	**73**
Day One in Australia	75
Bonding	76
Black and White Birds	77
Strange Policeman	78
Cannibals	79
Getting the Girl	80
Terms of Friendship	81
Giving Up Drinking	82
Miles From Home	84
Going Bush	85
Brawl	87
John's Dog	88
Fair Go	89

The Balmain Hippies	90
LSD	91
The Horse Trip	92
Head Monk	94
The Yellow Bag	95
Kindness of Strangers	96
Kookaburra	97

Magpies — 99

First Child	101
My Father	102
Fathering	103
Chemistry	104
Language	105
The Egg Came First	107
Gerard Jacks	109
Miklós	111
My Wife	112
The Kid's Religions	113
Little Girls	115
Shared Brain Cell	116
Pure Luck	117
The Practice of Art	118
Seeking Sanctuary	119
Who knows what people can bear?	120
My Mother	121
Lessons in Love	122
The Old-time Communist	123
Thanks	125
Wanting to Make Love to Her	126
Magpies	128
My Friend Death	129
Bread	130
Awakening	132

Postscript — 134

Author's note

Any likeness to persons living or dead is probably accurate but may be coloured by Ervin's memory and my poetic licence. I hold no responsibility for incorrectness of historical fact. The stories are anecdotal. I do hold responsibility for embellishment with details from my personal experience – for example, the nose prints of a pig or the dimensions of a stockman's hat. The names of persons not directly related to the protagonist have been changed.

Sparrow

Conception

I'm not really sure why my mother
was a Catholic nun. Perhaps she had
a spirituality that I knew nothing about.

I was told that in those days
the Hungarian gentry gave
their eldest daughter to the church.

Or maybe they wanted
to keep her away
from a certain Jewish man.

In any case she wasn't a nun for long;
my birth saw to that,
per-kind-favour a certain Jewish man.

Unwanted? You could say that,
unwanted by my father and certainly
unwanted by my grandmother.

When I refused to die
my grandmother had me fostered
to a peasant family.

I lived with the Mezeies for two years
before my mother came for me.

Going to Market

Wheels on gravel,
the clopping of hooves
in sweet morning air

scent of manure and earth,
steam from the horse's nose
as it nodded in its steady walk.

The cart moved forward
with a rhythmical sway
not so different from sleep.

On my left
the big warm bottom
of Mother Mezei.

Father Mezei on the right
held the reins
crooning to the horse.

Below the tree line
the sun
lingered awhile.

Small wild creatures
appeared and hid:
A rabbit, sparrows, fox cubs.

No one spoke.
The morning
was being morning.

Zsuzsi

Zsuzsi was big and pink
and loving and gentle
with her wet nose
and her friendly grunts.
Pigs can smile.
She stood as tall as me
and gave me little nudges
for a scratch on the back with a stick.
She rolled her eyes up
and pushed her back towards the stick
as she painted my legs
with nose prints.

One morning I awoke very early.
It was dark but I knew
I was alone in the house.
A dog barked from a distance.
Industrious noises rose from the yard.
Then I heard the pig yell, a high, unearthly squeal.
They had warned me that one day
they would butcher Zsuzsi.
The first grey light seeped into the sky.
Soon it would bloody the clouds.

Mud Cake

In the dirt on the street outside the house
I was making mud cakes with my pee.
A man shouted, 'Watch out little boy!'
and I looked up. A huge white dog
was lolloping down the street,
drooling at the mouth with rabies.
The running men cornered it
against a whitewashed wall
and split its head open with an axe.
A spurt of red sprayed up the wall.

My mud cakes tasted gritty.

The First Lie

The first lie that I remember
was told to me by my mother.

It was the day she took me from Mrs Mezei.
She said that they would leave the high window open

so that Mrs Mezei could get in when she came.
I knew she was lying. Mrs Mezei would not come.

Mrs Mezei was not my mother.
She was.

René

René zoomed me around the room.
My own giggle was the engine noise.
He even let me play with his model plane
although it was precious to him.

René was my stepfather for a little while.
With him my mother was happy.
He was swarthy, French
and my mother was petite, Hungarian.

René was French Resistance.
My mother was Communist.
I was a little boy.

But the Gestapo
did not discriminate.
They took us all.

The Cross

Behind the SS soldiers was the cross.
I comforted my mother when they shot René.
She was round with his child.
The baby rolled over in its watery world,
was born and named René.
Her heart held.

Behind the SS soldiers was the cross.
They dressed a Christmas tree for me
because I was the only child in the jail.
In the barracks, my mother put the little cake
on a high shelf next to my bed.
In the morning it was gone.

Behind the SS soldiers was the cross.
I comforted my mother
when they threw baby René in the fire.
I was three years old.
My mother was thin in my embrace.
Her heart, her heart,

I don't know what happened to her heart.

Snow

The soldiers took me to the yard.
They let me throw snowballs at them.
We got all powdered with snow
and laughed and laughed.
And because they were the enemy
and this was war
I threw those snowballs and I won.

Going to the Hitler Youth

They decided to put me
into the Hitler youth
but when they separated me
from my mother
I smashed the English toilet.

Water went everywhere
with little shards of ceramic.
I glowered with rage.
I was all teeth and claws.
They put me in a cell on my own.

A Shiny Stone

The German nurse scrubbed my ears
with a rough dry cloth and it hurt.

She took me to a room where my mother
knelt in front of me, and said,
'Ervin, it's me, Anna, your mother.'

I don't know how much time had passed
but I didn't feel for her, even outside
where the bombs were falling

Anna was a strange woman pulling me forward
and all I wanted was a particular shiny stone
from between the cobbles.

The Train

My mother had a little bag.
I had a little stone.

We were waiting on the siding for the train
that would take us back to Budapest.

Before you heard the engine of the train,
you could hear the wailing.

Injured soldiers were on the train
and they were returning home.

Budapest Hospital

In the corridors of the hospital
soldiers were begging to die.

They were in bags hanging from hooks
because they had no arms or legs.

My family was searching for itself
but none was wounded on the outside.

Orion's Belt

A child in post-war Budapest,
I had seen things no child should see.

I stood alone at the window of the barracks
with the immense night sky glittering above.

Three stars stood out in an orderly line
and I adopted those stars.

My stars, my little piece of security
a steady beacon in a life of uncertainty.

Beauty in strife, they shine for me
hope and clarity, even today.

Grandfather

Grandfather hid his whisky in my toys
when he took me to the park.
When we crossed the road
he held up his stick and walked
and the traffic stopped for him
just as he expected it would.

He dressed like a gentleman
with a cravat and cane.
They said, 'But Apa, it isn't the way
Communists dress.'
He said, 'I have dressed this way all my life
and the clothes should not go to waste.'

The doctors had told him
not to drink or smoke cigars
because it would kill him.
He was one hundred and four when he died.
He died because his wife yelled at him
for stealing his own whisky.

And all Grandmother could say was,
'But I caught him.'

The Washroom

Communism dealt with the wealth
and gave us a little washroom
at the back of a big house.

In order to make everyone equal
they made sure the formerly wealthy
had less.

My grandmother, mother and I
shared the small damp room.
We cooked and slept and bathed there.

At night the bedbugs would climb the walls
and my mother would kill them with a candle.

Meat

When a horse died
bolt upright
frozen solid in the street
people came
out from their homes
with meat cleavers
and axes
and hacked off
chunks of meat and ate well
for a few days.

Taking Advantage of the Situation

My mother didn't approve of stealing
but she warmed herself with the coal I supplied
and ate the food that I brought home.

I was very good at it
but I didn't call it stealing. I called it
'taking advantage of the situation'.

'That boy could steal the church bell,'
said my grandmother, tucking into the duck
that I'd taken advantage of at the zoo.

She didn't know she had given me an idea.
There was good money in metal on the black market
but I couldn't steal the church bell.

The lead gutters, on the other hand,
and the flashing – the local church
fed the poor for weeks.

Grandmother

My grandmother and I
had an all-out brawl when I was seven.
I had a nervous tic and she kept hitting me
as if I was doing it on purpose.

I threw the rolling pin over the back shed
after I'd put her to bed with it.

She never hit me again
but she would have killed me if she could
and in 1956 she nearly succeeded.

There was a curfew enforced by snipers.
They shot at anything that moved.
Dogs were found with bullets between the eyes.

I tried to shelter at my uncle's house
but grandmother threw me out again.
My uncle said, 'If he goes out there
he'll be killed.' But she insisted.

Spite kept her alive until she was ninety-six.
She died in hospital, mopping the floor
because she disapproved of the way
the cleaners were doing it.

A fitting end.

Of God and Oxen

My cousin Dodi could speak Latin.
He could have understood the Latin Mass
if he had gone to church.

I was an altar boy for a short while
before the Russians banned it.
Dodi gave me some pointers.

After the priest blessed the wine he would
take a sip and I was supposed to singsong
some Latin words that I didn't understand.

Dodi told me to sing instead,
'Quod licet iovi, non licet bovi.'
Which I did. Whereupon the priest kicked me.

Roughly translated, it means,
'What is allowed for Jupiter
is not allowed for the common ox.'

I lost my job.
It didn't matter.
Already, I did not believe in God.

Girls

Girls always got me into trouble.
Magda from next door would ask me
to climb the peach tree so that
she could look up my shorts.
I don't know why that was my fault.

Cousin Eva had me stand on top of a stump
to see if I could hit the fence with my piss.
When someone came, she said, 'Run!'
You try running from the top of a stump
with your penis in your hand in the middle of a pee.

Ági had me take it out in class. 'Show it to me,'
she said. If that happened in Australia now
I'd be counselled and mistrusted forever.
But the teacher just yelled, 'Put it away, Janek!'

The Doctor

Mother didn't know a lot about penises.
She didn't have one herself
and she was worried about mine.
So she took me to a doctor.
The doctor, who was female,
had a good look, lifted it up,
drew back the foreskin a little
and fondled it slightly. She smiled
at me and raised her eyebrows
as if to say, 'Lovely,'
then looked back at my mother
and said in a professional tone,
'This is an absolutely perfect penis.'

I shudder to think of all the ways
that could have gone wrong.

The Birthday Poem

Comrade Szèkely was all woman,
just the right amount of everything
in all the right places.
She was my teacher when I was nine
and I was her pet. Literally.
I would look at her, panting,
with my tongue hanging out and puppy-dog eyes.
When they were renovating the Women's
she chose me to guard her toilet.
Intimate.
Once when I was being cute
she hugged me to her belly and ruffled my hair.
The scent of her body
nearly made me swoon.

But one day she chose another boy to guard her toilet.
I was very angry.
I was so angry that when they chose me
to write a poem for her birthday, I refused.
I wrote one anyway and she caught me.
After she'd read it, she sent the poem (and me)
to the headmaster. He read it
and then stood at the window looking out.
I could see that he was stifling laughter.

The poem went,
I wish you
one hundred and fifty years of life
but let me be the one
to put the last wreath on your grave
so that I can watch
as your snow white bum soars skywards
getting hooked
on the horns of the wicked moon
and scalded red
by the sun.*

'So,' said the headmaster after a while,
'Is it possible that Comrade Janek
is in love with Comrade Zsèkely?'
'Yes, Comrade,' I said.
'And is it possible that Comrade Zsèkely
has disappointed Comrade Janek in some way?'
'Yes, Comrade,' I said. Then he gave me a spiel
about love, how there are disappointments.
'It hurts, but it's no use holding on. Better
to go for a walk, write some poetry, and forget her.'

So that's what I did.
The bitch.

---

* *I wish you...* was written by Ervin Janek when he was nine years old; translation by Ervin Janek and Belinda Broughton.

Sparrow

The Hefner brothers sold me the sparrow.
They had caught it in their street
and were taking it to school in a shoebox.
It cost me my lunch money.
'What are you going to do with it?' they asked.
'Eat it,' I said.

I didn't go to school that day.
I went down to the railway siding
where there was a bit of unkempt land.
Berry bushes in full white blossom,
daisies, dandelions, wild blue hyacinths,
there were even tulips from when
it had been a garden. It still looked
like a garden to me.

I held the sparrow for a moment,
the weightlessness of its body,
delicacy of feather and bone,
its small heart hammering against my finger.
Then I opened my hand and it was gone.

I had a whole spring day ahead of me.
And sunshine.

Dawn on Lake Balaton

In the dormitory of the school camp
my classmates slept.
The lake reflected the clean morning sky
as calm as a centre.

I was where I liked to be,
alone and in nature,
wading in the gloss of water,
reflection of sky.

Small birds were twittering,
bathing in sparks of light.
An egret high-stepped
his regal water-walk.

I found a mussel shell,
opalescent white, bright with light.
In the water it sank,
fluttering slow-motion side to side.

I dropped it
and it sank
again and again
like a feather in air.

Not Murder

The horse had no strength left; that was plain.
It stood leaning forward into the harness
against the weight of the over laden cart,
its white breath coming out in puffs, sweat a-lather.

At ten years old I thought the answer
would be to take some load off the cart
but the man's idea was to make a fire
underneath the horse.

He was bending over the kindling to set it ablaze
and there was no one else on the street to stop him.
So I picked up the heaviest rock
and heaved it onto the man.

It split his shoulder open and I
was shocked by the blood.
I ran for it. I was scared by how easy
it would have been to kill that man.

When I came back, the street was empty.
There was no horse, no man, no cart,
just a little heap of cinders
and some blood.

Árpád

When Árpád moved in with my mother,
I moved out – to the streets.
I was afraid of him. He was a big angry man
but also he was psychic.

Once I threw a plate at him and it was
a perfect shot. It flew straight at his head
and just in the last fifteen centimetres
it veered upwards and missed him.

Another time, a friend of ours
was tuning her flute. He asked her
what note she wanted and then
he pointed at his piano and it sounded.

I'm not kidding about this; it is true.
The Russians wanted him for research
into psychic phenomena but he refused.
You'd have to be psychic to refuse the Russians,

or mad, and he was both. Mostly he used it
to amuse himself and manipulate people,
my mother especially, I thought, but she loved him.
I hated him and the feeling was mutual.

He is the reason I spent a lot of nights sleeping
in public toilets and why I was so often hungry.
My mother was not the best provider
and I was not allowed to touch his food.

So I pissed in his pickles. It was such a joy
to watch him eat them with his stern ugly face
and salami grease on his chin.
It almost quietened my growling stomach.

During the uprising of 1956 I sheltered at their house.
I had a machine gun over my shoulder and he
was afraid of me even though it hadn't occurred to me
to hurt him. I guess he couldn't manipulate bullets.

When I went back in '93, Mother said, her voice
deep and sad, 'Árpád died, you know.' I nodded
and she said, 'His head blew up.' Apparently one side
of his head just burnt up, no external reason for it.

I believe it. My mother was incapable of lying.

Deer in the Woods

One night my neighbour was in our common walkway.
She was wearing a dark silken robe
over her voluptuous figure.
We boys fantasised about her in our crude way
discussing what we would like to do to her and how.
Of course we were virgins.

It was balmy
and the moon floated clear of the buildings
washing the ordinary scene with pale blue light.
I had been walking all day and reading.
I was drunk with poetry.

'Beautiful moon,' I said and she said,
'Ah, the moon. It's so romantic.'
'Like poetry,' I said and she asked
what I'd been reading and if I would recite some.
So I recited:

Innocent one
for your delight
I will behave as one
who cannot behave
any other way
but touching you
with playful touch
behold!
tonight we will be bold
as a deer in the woods
with its mate
and we will not

be ashamed because
we are blessed with wisdom
and with bliss*

whereupon she took my hand, led me inside
kissed me and undressed us both.
I said that I didn't know if women desired sex
or if it was just men's fantasies
but she assured me women love it too.

Afterwards she offered me a cup of tea
but I got shy suddenly and rushed off home.

**Innocent one…* is translated (with liberty) from memorised Hungarian by Ervin Janek and Belinda Broughton; title and author are unknown.

Comrade Várodi

When Stalin died, the whole of Hungary
was meant to stand for a minute's silence.
Comrade Várodi said that we could spend the minute
more comfortably on our backsides.

He was our literature teacher
and had already re-taught us how to lie.
'Make up stories,' he'd say. 'You surely know how to lie.
I loved literature, loved stories, loved words.
I would have become a writer if life hadn't intervened.'

When Comrade Várodi married he told us about
having to fight for the hand of his wife.
How his opponent was old-fashioned,
so it had to be a sword fight.

'Clack! Clack! Swish! Slash!' How he was cornered
at the bedroom door. (His true love was inside.)
How he took his chance and attacked and his opponent fell.
How he went through the door and locked it behind him…

'And?' I said, on behalf of the class.

'Don't you know?' he asked.
Not wanting to be embarrassed like that,
I said, 'If I was sure, I wouldn't ask.'
He said, 'Ask me when you matriculate.'

When we matriculated, we did ask him,
'So, what happened behind the bedroom door?'
and he replied, 'If you don't know by now,
you don't deserve your matriculation.'

Doves

Boots

They came for me in the middle of the night
just like in the movies.
The boots, the torch light in the eyes,
the glint of guns, the force in the hand
that gripped my arm.
'Be silent, get up, and get dressed.'

The interrogation room was typical too:
Grey, starkly lit, one desk, one chair
and one KGB official.
'Name?'
I was naive enough to think
that if I didn't say anything,
nothing could happen to me.
'Address?
Age?'

When I didn't answer the third time
the man got up as if he was being patient,
and walked around behind me.
He was only a small man but next thing
I was flying through the air. I hit the wall
and slid down it like a stunned bird.
Suddenly I remembered my name and address
and that I was sixteen and had been publishing
anti-Soviet poetry.

I thought that my tender age might help me
but they already had a file on me as thick as your wrist.
My tender age just meant I would be in jail
until they could try me as an adult.
And then, they suggested, sixteen years.

Bored Keepers

Jails are boring. It's one of their worst features.
Especially since the guards are bored too.

One day, when we were out
for our anticlockwise walk,
one dropped a cigarette in front of me.
I didn't dive for it like the others.
He said, 'Pick it up.
I said, 'I don't smoke.'
'Pick it up!'
He had a way of saying it
that made one realise
one has no choice
even though one knows the end
of this old joke.
I didn't even get the reward
of smoking the thing
after the good swift kick up the butt.

Another of their entertainments
was in the middle of the night.
They would bring prisoners together to fight.
You pretty soon learned
that at the click of the lock
you had to be on your feet and lay
whomever they brought out cold.
Otherwise it got dirty.

Happiness

The sun shone in
through the tiny high window of the cell

just a little slant of afternoon light
but it fell on the opposite wall

and filled the cell with light.
My skin, my hands,

I was turning them over in the light.
It felt like life.

The Opening of the Jail

When I'd been in jail for nine months
the most unthinkable thing happened.
There was a hell of a noise from the streets;
the city was shaking; guns were being fired.
Then a guard came along the corridor
with his keys and opened every cell.

He said, 'Go on! Get out of here! You're free!'
We all thought it was one of their tricks
and stood at the cell doors peeping out.
'Go on! Go! For God's sake just piss off!'
said the guard. Still no one moved.
So he pocketed the bullets
and slid his gun along the floor.

After we got our clothes, we all rushed out,
down the front steps of the jail and into
the throng of people. I was still fumbling
with the buttons of my coat.
I hadn't used buttons for nine months
and I remember every sensual moment
of pushing them through the holes
in the thick woollen cloth.

Then I was on the street and someone
put a machine gun in my hand.
'Come on, Son,' he said,
'Let's go and kill Russians.'
I was seventeen and I'd never killed
anything bigger than a flea in my life.

My eyes were still getting used to the light.

On Lenin Körút, Budapest, 1956

The crowd was throbbing on Lenin Körút
waving flags and chanting.
The nation was moving, surging
towards freedom, towards justice.

It was like one big organism
(a centipede perhaps?)
and moving forward
on its thousands of legs.

Years later I killed a centipede
in the outside loo.
And later I killed it again.
The family talked about it
and it turned out we had all killed it.
Centipedes never look dead.

But in this crowd people
were very definitely getting dead.
The Russian machine gunners
fired over their heads at first
but you can't stop a crowd like that.

There were only two machine-gunners
and the tank was cornered.
People fell but the crowd kept coming
through the blood tracking the blood
over the cobbles towards the tank.

The blood, the rage, and all those hearts throbbing
and they kept walking over the dead
and into the bullets
until they reached the tank
that they set fire to
and the men inside died.

Old Mrs Szabo

Old Mrs Szabo
used to give me cakes
when I was a child
and here she was
on Szegedi Utca
tearing the skin
from the corpse
of a KGB man
with her fingernails.

The National Guard

I wasn't cut out for the National Guard.
I had the papers and the machine gun
but I didn't like those rude captains,
or whatever they were, who kept barking at us.
On the first night's training we had to exercise
in the rain. Push-ups no less.
Then the captain, or whatever he was,
yelled instructions from underneath his umbrella,
to run to the produce market
and around the produce market
and back again and, no, we weren't allowed
to put down our rifles first.

When we got to the market
I forgot to turn right.
I kept running past the market
and on into the rain.
Someone was chasing me, though.
I could hear the footsteps
and he was catching up.
I figured I would be done for desertion.
Perhaps I should shoot him.
I was about as good at shooting people
as I was at turning right;
perhaps I could argue that
at my desertion hearing.

But then he yelled, 'Hey! Where shall we go?'
So we stopped and had a breather.

The White Coat

When the soldiers came to the hospital
I had just carried an injured man in.
The doctor put a white coat on me.
'See to this equipment, Doctor,' he said.

So I was pretending to adjust
a hanging bag of blood
with its little knobs and tubes
when the soldiers passed me by
without seeing my freedom fighter's boots.

Peer Pressure

One day, in the alley outside my mother's place
we met up with Rosa Hentés.
Butcher Rose by any other name.
Rose was his surname;
Butcher was the name people used
because he worked in the jail.

He was the one who softened new prisoners up.
He certainly knew how to hurt people.
I learned quite a lot from his administrations.
But he didn't get much from me; I was
just a stupid kid and had no useful information.
So he just made me watch.
He was very creative.
It was Butcher Rose's beautiful mind
that came up with the delightful torture
of pulling a prisoner's foreskin over a glass tube,
then breaking the tube.

This day, I was with a group of freedom fighters,
not people I knew well, but they knew I'd had dealings
with Butcher Rose. They looked at me.
'This is your man,' one said.
I looked at Butcher Rose.
He was unarmed and surrounded. He was frightened.
He wasn't the same man as in the jail.

I said, 'Oh, let's just go.'
'No,' said one of my group. 'This is your man.'
Silence for a moment, and then he said,
in a voice as hard as Butcher Rose's,
'THIS IS YOUR MAN'
so that I understood
it was him
or me.

So I shut my eyes and pulled the trigger.
I didn't see him falling.
I didn't see him dead.
I don't dream of him.
But I wish it was not my history.

Why to Not be Rude to Soldiers

A group of us were taunting soldiers
yelling at them
insulting their mothers.

No guns,
we only had spite
and sticks and stones.

But I went too close
and one of the soldiers caught hold of me.
He gave me to his friends

and they held me while he said,
'You talk too much,'
and aimed his boot at my face.

All my pearly whites
gone
just like that.

They left me on the street
and I didn't have much to say
for quite a while.

A Little Outing

A lot of the soldiers were Hungarians.
Their Russian superiors ordered them
to shoot at the people.

But these were their people, their kin,
and most of them refused to follow orders.
A lot of them deserted.

So the Russians left the city.
The people were jubilant.
Honestly, we thought we had won.

I don't remember how long they were gone
but one morning we woke up and they were back.
Snipers in place and the tanks rolling in again.

I knew the sewers and that's how I got to Gömb Utca
where my old friends Alex and Vincent and I
got on our pushbikes and went for a little outing

towards the border.

Running for the Border

We were hardly out of Budapest
when Alex got shot in the shoulder.
The soldiers loaded us and our bikes
into the back of their truck. One of them
handed me my bike by the machine gun
that was wrapped to the cross bar.

They brought us to the hospital
and took Alex in, but before they did
one of them looked me directly in the eye
and said, 'You boys stay here.'

And you know, Vincent would have.
He didn't realise it was an invitation.
I just about had to drag him out of the truck.
He didn't have it in him really,
neither the street savvy nor the desperation.

The next night on a bridge, soldiers found us
with their spotlights. 'Hey! You with the bikes,
come here!' and Vincent did. He just turned around
and walked back to them.

I threw my bike over the edge and jumped after it.
It took me three hours to creep away
through the undergrowth on the side of the creek,
the spotlights searching for me.
That was the last I saw of Vincent.

I caught up with Alex again in 1969. He refused
to talk about any of it, insisted it didn't happen.
It was OK for me, I suppose. I was Australian
but he still had to live with the ears in his walls.

When I came to the River Zala

the bridges were guarded
by machine gunners and tanks
but a local whispered,
'There is a boatman after dark
for a fee.'

And sure enough
after dark he came to the river
wiping his dinner from his moustache
and he told me
the price.

I said, 'I have no money.'
He looked at my broken face
spitting
chips of teeth
and at the machine gun across my chest
and he gestured to the boat
and I got in

and he rowed me
to the other side.

The Old Woman

Near the Pinka River, I knocked on a door.
An old woman opened it. 'Come in, son,' she said.
I said I just wanted directions but she
insisted I have some food and a little warmth.

I was sipping some bone broth
and softening bread in it, when we heard boots.
'This will be my grandson,' she said.
'He is a soldier but won't come in.
He doesn't want to catch anyone.'

'Evening, Grandma!' we heard.
'Everything all right?'
'Everything's fine, son,' she called
and the boots moved on.

She gave me directions to the river.
'Go straight that way,' she said, pointing
her crooked old finger. 'When you see a church
go to the left of it and cross the river there.
Don't go right or you'll end up back in Hungary.'

I went so straight that I climbed
an awkwardly high fence
only to look aside and see
an open gate not five metres away.

Then I settled down on the side of the river
to wait out the night. Stars and snow.
The water in constant movement
towards
        somewhere.

2 December 1956, Hungarian Border

I made my way
when dawn lit the river enough
to follow the old woman's instructions.
I edged my way in, naked,
my clothes and machine gun on my head,
and I started moving quietly across.
Some other fool behind me
ran for it, splashing into the icy water
and the guards on the bridge opened fire.
The bullets were bouncing off
the floating ice but I was out of reach
and I didn't look back,
so determined was I
and back was death.
The other bank was Austria and safe.
I shivered into my clothes
but before I walked on
I looked back as refugees always do.
I was alone with the brook
that separated me from my country.

My First Shave

Immediately after I crossed into Austria,
there was a loud noise, just something

being dropped, but my nerves were shot
from tension and exhaustion and I collapsed.

I woke up in hospital. They had removed
what were left of my teeth and given me a false set.

I was in a men's ward and a very beautiful nurse
was coming around shaving the patients.

When she got to me she said, 'How would you
like to be shaved?' and I said, 'Oh, just normal.'

So she very politely shaved my duck's fluff off.
She didn't say, 'There's nothing to shave,'

or anything like that. Just as well;
I was embarrassed enough already.

Speaking German

In the refugee camp, we ate in a big dining room.
Rows and rows of tables, with Austrian girls serving food.

One morning I called one over and asked for another
piece of bread. She said, 'Do you speak German?'

I replied, 'No. I just would like some more bread, please.'
Except that I said it in German.

I didn't even know I spoke German. I'd learned it
at three when my mother and I were prisoners of war.

They'd put me in the Hitler Youth
and it was all I spoke for however long I was there.

Then my grandmother and mother
kept the language alive for me

by speaking it whenever they didn't want me
to understand what they were saying.

I'd sit under the table and they'd go on about things
that mothers and daughters talk about.

I guess you could say they educated me.

Eating with Knives

Hungarians eat with knives. It's what we do.
We get thick lumps of bread and bits and pieces
of speck, cheese, pickles and peppers
and we make our sandwiches in our mouths.
It's very efficient, but there are a lot of sharp knives.
Everyone's got one, usually a pocketknife.

When you are well fed you forget
that you've ever been starving.
At least most people do.
There was an older man in the refugee camp
and one day, for a joke,
I stabbed a piece of speck from his board
and put it in my mouth.
Next thing I was on the ground
and he had his knife to my throat,
its thin edge against the skin.

Someone pulled him off.
Needless to say, I never did that again.
He'd spent time in the Gulag.
It was every man for himself in the Gulag
and that man had survived.

The Monastery

I was a lost boy: no home,
cut off from my past, from my family
(such as it was) and my heritage.
So when the priest visited the refugee camp
and we got talking, I thought
becoming a monk could give me
a place to belong, a community,
and I joined the monastery.

I got off on the wrong foot the very first day.
Another young monk showed me to my cell.
Above the head of the bed was a bleeding Christ,
quite a large heavy one, and I picked up the pillow
and moved it to the foot of the bed.
'Why did Brother do that?' asked the other monk.
I said, 'In case He falls on me.'
No sense of humour – the monk reported me
and I had to do penance for my lack of respect:
so many lashes of self-flagellation.

I really wasn't cut out to be a monk.
I had no intention
to leave my willy alone for a start
and I didn't think that was so bad
that I needed to lash my back.
My little whip collected dust.
They didn't like my reading matter either:
Thomas Mann's *Magic Mountain* and Goethe's *Faust*.
It didn't take me long to realise
that I just didn't have a calling.

It isn't as easy to leave a monastery as it is to join.
I had to pray for twenty-four hours, out loud.
Every time I thought I could have a little rest
because the attending monk was snoring,
he'd wake up and say, 'Brother is to continue.'

At the end I kissed the priest's ring for the last time
and they showed me to a little room
with a door to the outside world.
All my worldly possessions were there:
my clothes, my two books and my little bag.

When I was dressed
I went to the door and opened it.
It opened onto nothing, into space.
It was so high above the ground
that you felt you would fall out
into the stark natural world
where there was no path.

I jumped. 'Let me out of here,' I thought.
'Oh, look at the world,
completely wild and godless.
How wonderful.' And off I went,

making my own path.

Sport-heart

My reputation preceded me
to George's Riding School in Salzburg.
I'd trained for steeplechase in Hungary
and had the build and strength of a jockey,
the will, and whatever it is that passes
between horse and man when their intents meet.

Also I bore the name Janek
and the horse that my grandfather rode to fame
still stands in the museum in Hungary.
Kincsem by name. Stuffed like Phar Lap.

In Austria I rode for Baroness Eliza Mernhoff
but soon I realised I was not just her jockey,
I was her toy. She liked to flaunt me in public,
took me to dinners where there was more cutlery
than you could count and toffs everywhere.

I preferred the company of horses.
I loved the power of a horse, the speed, the strength, the urge.
I loved the lift of the jump, the thunder of the race
but mostly, their individual characters.

But it all came undone the last time that I fell off.
I was used to broken bones. I had five from previous falls.
But this was different.

The problem was not four more broken bones.
The problem was losing consciousness,
not when I fell, before I fell. It was why I fell.
The horse and I were gathering for a jump, then – nothing.

Sport-heart, the doctor said. Heart murmur in English.
But I couldn't trust myself again, not with the life of a horse.
They had to kill that one.

Baroness Eliza Mernhoff and Her Horse

Baroness Eliza Mernhoff
really enjoyed her riding.
She looked spectacular
on a horse, at one with it,
a good seat, as they say.

A very good seat
I discovered once
when I happened upon her
riding alone in the stadium
– beautiful to watch.

The horse just coming into sweat,
every muscle shining,
arched neck, intent eye.
His rhythm like liquid
under Baroness Eliza Mernhoff's
trim backside. And that backside
also a liquid movement
of rhythmical muscles building
into the taut spasms of orgasm
that arched her back and flushed her face.
The horse flared his nostrils, tossed his head
and rolled back his eyes a little.

Then they settled down into a modest trot
and I made myself scarce

Doves

Where the horse manure,
rank and steaming, melted the snow

doves would come on their thin feet
to peck at the undigested grain.

I understand how they came
to be a symbol of peace

with their domestic colours
and soft voices

how they love
with such devotion

how watching them
can heal a war-torn heart.

I threw fresh seed or crumbled bread
and they came pecking

and crooning their one soft syllable
hoo, hoo

a sound one makes for a lover
or whispers into a baby's ear.

Decisions

I had a lot of options in the refugee camp.
First of all I could earn money as a translator.

I was also offered a job as a spy
if I just wanted to pop back to Hungary
and keep the nice gentlemen posted
on what the Russians were doing now.

Some people disappeared from the camp
so it was my aim to get
as far away from Hungary as possible.
There were fourteen countries
that would accept us,
so I took a look at the other side of the globe
and chose Australia.

Of course, there was more to it than that.
Australia was actively seeking immigrants.
They actually had glossy brochures
showing Australian life:
beaches, families having picnics,
mums in kitchens, baking.

They told us Australia was a new country
and needed the workforce.
We were told we could work for two years,
become Australian, then we could all
build a new nation together.

Music to the ears of a young man
searching for a future.

Kookaburra

Day One in Australia

When we got to Melbourne we were allowed
to get off the boat and have a look around
before they put us on the train to Bonegilla.

It was Sunday but Melbourne city was like a ghost town,
the heat rising off the pavements and no one in sight.

Not a toilet either and we were bursting.
So eventually we pulled them out and had a pee
near some steps going underground.

How come the only car in the street was a police car?

I don't remember how we got the message through
that we were from the boat but eventually
they took us there and got an interpreter for us.

Apparently baring your willy is called
'indecent exposure' and it's illegal
to piss on the streets in Australia.

We told the translator to tell the kind policemen
that we wouldn't have pissed on the street
if they had public toilets in Australia.

To which we were told,
'You pissed on the public toilets.'

No one had told us that toilets were called 'Men'
or that they were underground in Melbourne.

Bonding

The train travelled north,
past backyards of Melbourne
where washing hung on lines
and dogs panted under lean-tos.

We travelled through hectares and hectares
of farming lands, the train clacking and clunking,
before it stopped at a railway siding
and we had to get out.

There was nothing there, no buildings,
nobody to meet us, just a huddle of refugee
with our little bags in the middle of the bush
and the sun going down.

'They did say it was a new country,'
someone joked. 'Looks like we start
with building shelter.
Anyone bring an axe?'

It was about then, amongst all that rabble,
that I fell for gum trees,
such sensual creamy bark like the skin of women
ecstatic shapes in the dry yellow grass.

I never felt out of place in the Australian bush,
not even alone and miles from anywhere.
After a while some buses came for us
and they took us in to Bonegilla.

Black and White Birds

On my first morning in Bonegilla I woke early
and stood at the door of the cabin looking
out of the window at the sunshine, green grass,
and some black and white birds strolling around.

They were cocking their ears to the ground
and stabbing their beaks into the moist grass,
then throwing back their heads and singing –
tumbling notes into the clean morning air.

The fellow I was sharing a room with woke up.
He was about twenty-five and thought
he was so clever. 'What's that?' he asked,
half asleep and panicky.

'Oh, that,' I said. 'Haven't you heard
of the famous Australian singing snakes?
Very poisonous and aggressive apparently.'
That fellow didn't like me much either.

Strange Policeman

One day Gyurge and I were driving along the road talking at each other (as Hungarians do) or singing songs or something, when a policeman came up on the driver's side with his little light flashing and yelled at me, 'Pull over, Driver.'

I looked at Gyurgy and Gyurgy looked at me, and we shrugged.

I yelled back at the cop, 'No pullover,' but the cop yelled louder, 'PULL OVER, DRIVER!'

He was getting angry, I could see that, so I stopped the car and Gyurgy and I looked at each other again.

The policeman got off his motorbike and rearranged his balls and walked towards us like a bear, swaying from one leg to the other. He didn't get to open his mouth before I was trying to tell him I didn't have a pullover.

'No pullover,' I'm saying. 'Too hot for pullover. Shirt. Police no take shirt! Mine shirt!' and I'm pulling at my collar.

Gyurgy understood more English words than I did and he said the policeman said words like 'licence' and 'speed' and 'miles per hour'. But I just kept saying, 'No pullover!' and telling him he couldn't have my shirt, he had no right to my shirt and other things like that with a few Hungarian words thrown in also.

The policeman pointed at my speed dial and yelled at me, 'SLOW DOWN!' like I was deaf. Then he shook his head and got back on his motorbike and rode away.

Gyurge and I looked at each other again. We both understood what 'Slow down' meant but we couldn't go slower. We were stopped.

Cannibals

When I first went to the Northern Territory, someone kindly told me that the local Aborigines were cannibals. I didn't believe them and went out walking in the bush as I've always done even when I was a kid in Hungary.

One beautiful day – the sun dropping, painting everything with warm light: the orange grass, red soil, dark green leaves on the sensual ghost gums – I found a nice log to sit on and I lit my pipe. I used to smoke a pipe so girls would take me seriously. It didn't work then and it hasn't worked since.

So I was puffing away like an inflated toad when suddenly I heard it – the Aborigines, laughing. And what a spooky laugh: koo koo koo kaa kaa kaa, koo koo koo kaa kaa kaa.

They were all around me but I couldn't see them. Of course by that time I was on the ground stuffing dirt in my pipe to put it out. I kept lying there and they kept laughing and then – silence.

After a while, I began creeping quietly on my stomach until I figured I was far enough away to run like hell.

Back at camp I told the other Hungarians, 'I heard the Aborigines. They were having some sort of ritual. They must be cannibals.'

After that I was really wary of going bush but one day I was fishing with some friends, sitting on the bank of the South Alligator River, and that laughter started up again. My hackles were up and I was all over goose bumps. I thought we were done for.

But I looked over my shoulder and saw that the laughter was coming from a bloody bird and I said, cool as you like, 'You know, when some people hear that bird, they think it's the Aborigines coming to get them.'

Getting the Girl

Back when I was learning English, I was on a train from Tennant Creek to Darwin. There was an old stockman on the train, one of those tall thin men who probably had only three things in his life: cigarettes, work and drink. Oh, and maybe women, but not too often. Those stockmen roll up the sides of their hats so they can fit through doors.

Anyway, he was coughing his guts up. I hate to think what he had, TB maybe, or smoker's cough, something lethal. Every time he drew breath after one of the coughing fits, he'd sit back in his chair and say, 'Die, you bastard. Die.' So I filed that phrase away. You never know when you'll need a phrase like that. Poor old fellow, he made it to Darwin.

In Darwin in those days, everyone met everyone in the pub. Maybe they still do. The smell of beer and the cool air would flow out of those half doors and pool around your legs on the pavement. No wonder you went in. Bending your elbow was about all you wanted to do in heat like that and I'd been four months out bush, mining. That Friday there was a girl there. She was goddess material but she didn't know it. And apart from her looks, she was female.

I was trying to amuse her in my broken English. She was getting more light-hearted as she drank her Bundy and Coke, but then it went down the wrong way and she spluttered and coughed.

'Die, you bastard. Die,' I said.

She said, 'What?'

I repeated it, all eager and pleased with myself. 'Die, you bastard. Die.'

I got the girl. She taught me a lot of English, starting with 'God bless you.'

Later we traded English lessons for sex, a good deal whichever way you look at it.

Terms of Friendship

Greg used to call me 'Bastard'.
He'd say, 'Pass the wrench, you bastard,' or
'You're a bit early, you bastard,' or
'Comin' to the pub, you bastard?'

I asked him about it and he said,
'I call you Bastard because you're me mate.'
I wasn't sure how to use the word
so I looked it up in the dictionary.

That didn't answer any questions;
it just brought up two more,
namely: how did he know,
and why was he rubbing it in?

Giving Up Drinking

I gave up drinking when I stopped being a poet
or perhaps it was the other way around.
I used to drink a bottle of Johnny Walker a night
and sit in candlelight writing long ballads
in Hungarian.

Once my mate Sandor and I
went into the employment office
in dove grey suits with white roses on our lapels,
Goethe hats and walking sticks too.
The lady behind the counter asked how she could help us.
We said, 'We are looking for work.'
'OK,' she said, 'What do you do?'
'We are poets,' we said.
'Oh,' she said.
'Hungarian poets,' we added.
She said she didn't think they had a lot of work
for Hungarian poets and then walked through the divide
between the cubicles and called, 'Hey, Dave,
I've got a couple of poets here. Got any work for poets?
They're Hungarian poets.'
She came back with a very straight face and said,
'No, we have no work for Hungarian poets.'

Anyway, all that whisky didn't do me much good.
I went to the doctor and said,
'Hey, Doc, I'm not sure what's shaking, my hands or my head.'
The doctor said, 'Everything's shaking
and if you don't stop drinking,
it won't be shaking for long.'

When I got sober and read the poetry
I thought it wasn't very good
and it was in Hungarian.
So I burnt the lot.

Miles From Home

'This is the end of the line,'
said the bus driver
and I surfaced.

He stood in the aisle in front of me,
a large-bellied man with a kind face,
a gentle eye.

I was sitting in a pool of sweat,
my hands numb with clenching
and I was still shaking. I looked around.

There was no one else on the bus:
no KGB operatives, no spies,
no soldiers with machine guns.

This was Australia and everything was OK
except that I was miles
from my flat, miles from home.

Going Bush

1

My friend warned me, 'They have called the nuthouse. They will have you committed.'

My screaming nightmares and erratic behaviour had everyone concerned – even me. But I had read *The Manufacture of Madness* by Thomas Szasz and I didn't trust nut houses.

So I packed a few things into my Ford Customline and I split. In Darwin I swapped the Customline for an aluminium dinghy and a short-wheelbased Land Rover and I went bush. I travelled by setting up camp in one place, then walking around until I found another good camp, and then I drove there. I lived on fish and kangaroos.

2

That's beautiful country, Arnhem Land: clean water, healthy animals, no people. Or rarely. Sometimes I would see Aborigines. Their kids would come and check me out with their shy and curious eyes. I gave my watch to one once; he was so pleased. But he came back a few days later, saying, 'Watch no good. Too shiny.' Apparently it would glint when he was hunting and scare the animals away.

When the wet season came, I shared the bluffs with the Aborigines. There was plenty of room for us all. Sometimes I'd give them a lift in the Land Rover. There was one very old fellow who didn't trust vehicles. He wouldn't let go of his spears. Eventually we travelled along with him holding onto them out of the window but it took us quite a while to work out how to shut the door without him having to let go of them for a second.

I loved their sense of humour. They would tell me stuff with the straightest face, and when it finally dawned on me and I said, 'You're pulling my leg,' they would all fall about laughing.

I once asked one young man how far to somewhere. He said, 'Oh, not very far, few minutes' walk, couple a thousand miles.'

3

Sometimes my past would come and haunt me, the injustice, the pain, the lack of love. And one day I got angry. Why hadn't someone looked out for me? Then I did something that I later found out is used by psychologists. I adopted myself. Whenever I had a memory in which that little boy was mistreated, I stood up for him and gave him love. It all sounds very contrived, but it worked.

That, the solitude and the bush.

Brawl

One night in a pub a huge sweaty nasty man
decided he wanted to fight me.
'You come on outside, wog,' he said.
John said, 'You can't fight him. He's just a little fella.'
'I wanna fight the wog!' he said, muscles rippling
all over his chest and arms. This bloke had muscles
for eyeballs. Certainly he had meat inside his head.

John said, 'You're just a bloody brute.
Look at the size of you. You can't fight him.
Fight me.' But the brute wouldn't have it.
It was me he wanted. I told John
not to worry about it. 'He'll kill you,' said John
and he and half the pub came out
to watch the brute kill the wog.

The brute hitched his shorts up above his bum crack,
rearranged his singlet and was bobbing around
like a theatre boxer. He took a swipe at me.
I dodged it and then I laid him out cold.
'Where'd you learn to do that?' asked John.
'In year four,' I said.

From then on, John was my biggest worry.
He'd get a few beers into him and then he'd say,
'Anyone want to fight my little woggy friend here?'

John's Dog

John's parents had sold their old home.
They couldn't take all the animals
so John had to shoot his own dog.

He took the rifle and the dog and he set off into the bush.
He was walking along with the gun over his shoulder
calling the dog over every now and then, ruffling its ears.

Then he stopped, put the end of the rifle
to the dog's head. The dog looked up at him,
full of innocence and trust, and, bang, it was dead.

John put his rifle on the ground,
knelt down, buried his face in the dog's fur
and wept, sobbing like a child.

I high-tailed it home so he wouldn't know I knew
and when he came in he was dry-eyed.
'Job done,' he said, hanging up the rifle.

Fair Go

When I was logging
there was a bloke there called Bill.
He used to grab me by the hair
and pull me around, saying,
'Look! I got myself a wog here.'
I was fair game, he reckoned,
because I'm short. I was under
this bloody oaf's hand saying,
'Let me go, you prick, it hurts.'
And he was saying, 'Oh, listen
to the wog whine, "It hurts, it hurts."'
But he hadn't got the measure of me,
and next thing he was on the ground
with a broken wrist, crying like a baby.
I wasn't brought up on the streets
for nothing, but I thought, 'I'm dead.'
All his friends were standing around
and they were bigger than him.
So I was looking around like a cornered dog,
but not one of them moved.
He deserved it, they reckoned.
Fair go, they reckoned.

The Balmain Hippies

In Balmain we had a share-house where we got stoned, worked as little as possible, and made music and love. We dressed in loose, colourful clothes and grew our hair so that we could keep flowers there. Therefore we called it a hippy commune.

It was fun until I began saving to go to Europe. I needed to work and suddenly the all-night parties were a bit much. So I put a coin into my bedside lamp underneath the globe and, when I needed to shut them up, I'd give them fair warning and then I'd blow the fuses. No wonder they thought I had powers.

At the time we were all meditating to destroy our egos and become gods. We would talk Eastern mysticism and write haiku and be so stoned that everything was cosmic. Unfortunately some of the others wanted a guru and they began to treat me like one, nodding profoundly to anything I said, even stupid jokes and tripe. Probably it was because of the bedside lamp.

So I left. I had one hundred and fifty dollars and a ticket on a boat to Singapore. I wanted to see my mother in Hungary but I wasn't in any hurry. It took me over a year.

Nine months later I was sitting in a café in Herat, Afghanistan, when the hippies from Balmain walked in, accompanied by their guru. He was a Westerner and he began talking his cosmic spiritual rubbish at me.

I was very non-committal. I just kept saying, 'Hmm,' and wishing he would go away and stand on his head or something, when suddenly he cracked.

He began yelling at me. Then he threw the table over and stormed out.

'Hmm,' I said, and righted the table. I apologised to the owner of the café but he just nodded and smiled and said, 'Hmm.'

LSD

My first slip of LSD didn't work
so I took another.
It didn't work either so I went to bed.
I turned back the sheets
and sat on the edge of the bed,
straightening the pillow when
my brain fell out, pink and blubbery,
onto the white pillow slip.
'Well!' I thought and proceeded
to have a good look, an inspection
of the works so to speak.

The last time I took LSD
was also because of the bed.
I foolishly lay on it to rest.
It's best not to give the subconscious
the upper hand, I suppose,
because I woke in terror
to an Arabic number one in flames.
I was so frightened that I yelled out
and the pain stayed in my chest
for six months.

But in the meantime
it rearranged my life's pain.
It loosened me up,
cured my loneliness,
broadened my world view
and allowed me to dance.

The Horse Trip

Different music would change the mood
of LSD trips. If I wanted a light trip,
I would listen to Saint-Saëns' *Carnival of the Animals*,
to the Beatles if I wanted a psychedelic trip,
or, if I wanted to wallow in cathartic pain,
I would listen to Shostakovich's *Rite of Spring*.
But I don't remember if I had any music
to the horse trip.

There was a battle on my wall:
men with swords and Rah!
All very aggressive and beautiful,
Caravaggio's light and Rubens' animals.
But such violence.
It was too much for me.
I got up and walked between the horses,
pushing them aside, saying,
'Stop this fighting. Enough. Be peaceful.'
The horses' necks were sweaty and thick with muscle,
bumpy with pumping veins.
It was noisy with the clatter of metal,
the clopping of hooves.

During re-entry that day
I sat on the front step of the house at Balmain.
It was warm and peaceful because everyone was out.
I could smell the horses on my hands
and I thought, 'That's just a shadow.'
Sometimes things like that
would follow you into your life for a little while.

But when Terry came home, dragging his arse
through the gate, his workday exhaustion on his face,
I said, 'Terry, smell this,' and held up my hand.
'Phew!' he said. 'You been among horses?'
I didn't answer and he lumbered inside.

What was that? How did he know? Don't answer.
For forty years I have not asked that question
because no one can answer it.

Head Monk

In the '60s the Buddhist temples in Asia
couldn't turn you away if you asked for refuge.
There were a lot of stoned Westerners taking advantage.

I once witnessed a couple having sex
on the altar of a holy sanctuary.
There was a young monk watching,
his head on the side like a curious pup.

I stayed at a monastery in Singapore for four months.
I asked the head monk for some work to earn my keep.
I served the monks their one meal each day.

The head monk was as fat and happy
as any Buddha should grow.
In the afternoon he would sip tea
and talk to me about all sorts of things.

One time I asked him, 'What about Jesus Christ?'
This sweet funny man suddenly morphed into a Western hippy,
'Hey, Man! If Jesus Christ's your man, then Jesus Christ's your man.'

When we had dried our tears of laughter, I asked again,
'But really, what do you think of Jesus Christ?'
'Not much,' he said. 'I don't think much of Buddha either.
Jesus was an enlightened man. We call him a Buddha.'

The Yellow Bag

I went with a monk far into the forest.
We walked for hours chatting now and then
but once we got to the river he crossed his legs
and that was the end of conversation.

After a few hours I realised
I was not capable of sitting still for three days
and so I started back
through the dense forest with its brimming life.

Then night came on and I had to settle down
amongst the strange sounds, in complete darkness.
There was nothing but a foreboding sense
of life consuming life and, of course, tigers.

Some time before morning, I thought, 'Oh well,
if this is the way I go, this is the way I go,'
and I slept, waking up in the morning, alive!
The head monk laughed himself to tears.

Then he took his yellow embroidered monk's bag
and hung it on my shoulder. 'For you,' he said
and was suddenly serious. 'But don't
flash it in India. It could get you killed.'

Kindness of Strangers

If you see a sign that says,
'Water Unsuitable for Human Consumption',
it is unwise to wash your grapes there.
Especially if you have not taken your hepatitis tablets.

Naturally I nearly died. I hitchhiked to Kabul in the back
of a fish truck sliding around on top of the fish, covered, as I was,
in shit and flies, and woke up in the hospital with someone
waving a paper in front of me, saying, 'Sign here.'

The man in the next bed said, in quiet English,
'Do not sign that paper. It says they do not
have to take responsibility for you. They will
let you die.' So I did not sign that paper.

There was a little boy with a goat in the room.
He was trying to swap the goat for the life of his brother.
It seemed the doctor did not need a goat
but I slept before I heard the outcome.

When I woke, they were getting me ready to fly to Teheran.
The man in the next bed reached over. 'Take these,' he said.
'They will bring you luck,' and he pressed into my hand
some Islamic worry beads much smoothed with prayer.

It isn't often in your life that you receive a pure gift,
one from a stranger whom you will never meet again.
The man was older than me. He will have died by now.
But his heart is still warming my pocket.

Kookaburra

I slipped into the Budapest zoo
through the gap in the fence
that I'd used as child.

A grown man,
I felt a little embarrassed
but I didn't get caught.

I know that these days,
zoos do good work saving species
whose habitat we've ruined,

but a zoo is a zoo
and in the Budapest zoo
there was a kookaburra.

He was not laughing.
not preening
not glinting his mean eye.

He was not looking around.
He was just sitting still
with his head lowered.

Suddenly I knew I was Australian.
This was my bird and it was an atrocity
that he was caged.

I would have let him out
if there had been anywhere
to fly to.

Magpies

First Child

In my arms lay
the purest being
I had ever seen.

A sleeping face
more peaceful
than any Buddha.

In fact, he was a Buddha
and it was my fatherly duty
to not stamp him

into the mould
of civilised morals
or domesticated human.

Of course
it would happen anyway because
we are human.

But in the meantime it was my job
to look into that wizened face
and learn.

My Father

As a little kid I would make up stories
about my hero father who died in the war,
but the two times I met my father,
he was no hero. He was drunk
and surrounded by an arrangement
of beautiful women from whom
he didn't exactly hold back.
He gave me a few *forint* each time
but I can't say I thought too much about him
after I was nine.

When I was thirty-five I took my first wife
to meet him. I thought, 'I'll go and show off
my pretty young wife to my old father.'

He was so like me it was embarrassing.
Not that we looked alike, but we told similar jokes,
gesticulated the same way, even used
the same (unusual) turns of phrase.
It was like watching someone impersonate me.
So much for the nature/nurture debate.
So we sat around, shocked,
speechless in the presence of our selves,
when his very beautiful wife came in.

She was nineteen.

Fathering

I had a son with each of my first two wives.
The first wife fell in love with her boyfriend,
the second with her girlfriend, but the boys
stayed with me. We licked our wounds.

Funny how you try to protect them –
these little drops of your blood,
out in the huge raw world – so vulnerable.
They sneeze in another country and you can feel it.

The world comes with its spiders and cliffs,
its friends of the heart and foes of the heart,
and it takes them, wide-eyed with excitement.
They plunge willingly into the unknown waters.

There's not a thing you can do to protect them
but before you know it, two men stand next to you,
as solid as the rocks
that they skinned their knees upon.

Chemistry

When my first son was born, I thought,
'This drifting from job to job is not for a married man.'
So I enrolled to train as a biological lab technician.
I did quite well except I just didn't get chemistry.
I couldn't fathom it at all.

I had a wonderful teacher called Barry Gillic.
He tried his hardest, gave me extra tuition.
It didn't help, but Barry became a good friend.

When my first wife left, he came visiting every night.
I was destroyed by the break-up. I thought in marriage
you just stuck together. But suddenly I was on my own
with a three-year-old who was asking for his mother.
One day he said, 'When will Mum come home?'
and I said, 'I don't think she will live with us again,'
and my little boy's bowels moved into his corduroy pants.

Anyway, Barry would come every night and try
to get chemistry to stick in my brain.
I needed to pass it to get the certificate
even though Barry said I'd never need it.
'You will be a technician, not a professor.'

Exam day came, and we all filed into the room.
I'd been throwing up, I was so nervous.
But Barry had put huge posters up on the walls
so that we could look up the answers.

And when he handed me my paper I opened it and saw
that he had filled it out, cleverly too; I got a bare pass.
Afterwards I said, 'You didn't have to do that Barry,'
and he said, 'Yes, I did.'

Language

I learnt English from miners and I had friends
like Don, who taught Dirk rhymes like
'Donald Duck had a fuck
Donald Duck got stuck
Bad luck, Donald Duck'
Probably not what one should teach a four-year-old.

Even so, I saw red when I came in to pick Dirk up
from childcare to find him standing in the corner.
Whenever anyone came close, he would turn around
and say, 'Fuck, fuck, fuck, fuck, fuck, fuck, fuck.'
with his little face screwed up like a demon.

The teacher told me, 'Dirk has a problem with
his language. He has been standing in the corner
all day because of his swearing.
Where do you think he picked it up from?'

This woman spoke in one of those affected
upper-crust accents that make you want to puke
especially if your little boy has been standing
in the corner all day. Usually I didn't swear any more
but I said, 'Fucked if I know, Love, and fucked if I care,
but you fuck off right now and get my child.'
'Mr Janek!' she said.

So I found another centre.
I explained that Dirk swore a lot.
'Oh, they all do that, Mr Janek,' said the carer.
'Just ignore it. It will go away.'

All went well at this centre until a few days later.
I was coming in and I saw Dirk come
flying down the hill on a tricycle, hit a hole
and nearly fall off, whereupon he yelled out
at the top of his voice, 'Did you see that, Lisa?
I nearly went arse over tit in that fucking hole!'
and I thought, 'Uh oh, here we go again.'

But Lisa just smiled and said, 'Did you, Dirk?'
And as promised, he stopped swearing at all
after a few months.

The Egg Came First

'What's white when it goes up and yellow
when it comes down?' I asked my four-year-old.
'What?' he said. 'Come and I'll show you,'
and we walked out to the front pavement.
Just then a bus full of commuters pulled up at the stop
and they saw a perfectly serious man and boy
throw an egg up in the air,
watch it hit the gutter
and then walk back inside.

We also dissected his canary when it died.
I didn't know what else to do, seeing the tears welling.
'I wonder why it died.' I said, 'Shall we find out?'
So out came the dissecting kit and away went the tears.
We inspected the innards of the bird as if they were a puzzle,
came to some sort of conclusion,
and then we buried it with full flowers and honour.

So Dirk got into experimentation.
His main area of inquiry was fire and bombs.
One day there was one hell of a bang in the backyard.
I came scrambling out of my workshop
to find two little white-faced boys
rolling on the ground with laughter.
The little fire they had lit was burning merrily
and the aerosol can they had heated
rocked quietly beside the iron fence.

He even talked his year nine science teacher
into making an elaborate device
involving match heads and a soda stream bottle.

He sold it to the teacher by discussing
the 'electronic launching device'.
So the class went out to the oval
where the electronic launching device definitely worked,
launching the soda stream bottle with an almighty boom
to who knows where? It was never seen again.

Dirk is thirty-nine now. His wife tells me
that recently, at one of their parties, he and a friend
lit one of those tennis balls on a string
and then proceeded to have a spectacular spinning game
until the string burnt through
and the flaming ball ricocheted off into the night,
off into someone else's backyard.

I guess we can blame at least part of it on the egg.

Gerard Jacks

When I couldn't get a job in my profession, I decided to work
for myself. I had done some woodwork in Germany
so I thought, 'Toys: I'll give them a go.'
I produced a few items and began selling to shops.

One shop owner, called Gerard Jacks, got very excited
about my toy train. It disassembled into a neat little box.
Gerard and I went into partnership although
I pretty soon realised what that meant.
It meant I did the work and Gerard made the money.
He was a total rip-off artist. He even told me his maxim,
'Don't pay any bill until they ring you and then dispute
the amount.' He said you can get a hundred and twenty days
credit that way. It was exactly how he treated me.
One day he came to the workshop and there was sawdust
everywhere. Gerard grabbed a broom and, in a rage,
began sweeping. His wife took me aside and said,
'I'll ring you before we come if you like
so you can clean up first.' I just laughed and said,
'Now why would I do that, Hildika? Sweeping suits him.'

Eventually I ended it. I withdrew half of the money
in our joint account and went to tell Gerard it was over.
'Oh,' he said, frowning. He thought for a little while
and then said, 'How about I give you three hundred dollars.'
'Sure,' I said, 'that would be lovely,' and home I went
to await the telephone call. Sure enough a few hours later,
Gerard was on the phone ranting, 'You withdrew the money!'
'Only my half of it, Gerard,' I said.
'But you let me give you three hundred dollars!'
'Oh,' I said, 'did you think that was my share?

Fancy that. I thought you were being generous.'
He used some expletives but he was laughing;
he hated to lose money even when it wasn't his,
but he knew when a joke was on him.

Miklós

His mother promised me a dark-haired, brown-eyed, introverted little girl but Miklós was born squawking, red-faced and very definitely a boy. His eyes are as blue as a summer sky and he is wholeheartedly noisy, always beating a tune or singing.

When he was young, it was advertisements; it used to drive us nuts. He made a study of television – advertisements, trivia and movies – but in between threw water bombs at cars or explored mine shafts. He was very good at being naughty.

His mother left when he was five but she came for dinner on Wednesdays and he spent weekends with her. It's hard for kids moving from house to house.

When he was a teenager, the house was full of hulking young men and the fridge was always empty. When they ate a whole week's groceries in one night, we had to put a stop to it. 'We can't feed the village,' I said.

He was a very imaginative child, fascinated by the unexplainable. He devoured documentaries and books on alien abduction, spon-taneous human combustion and altered states of consciousness and had the nightmares to match.

As a teenager he altered his own consciousness with whatever he could find and left home at seventeen to drift. Everyone worried except Belinda, who said, 'Didn't you do that? Didn't I? Just wait, he'll come through.'

And he has. He is settling now, wants kids, and we think he has met his match. All that television paid off too. He is a filmmaker.

My Wife

Someone mentioned her before we met and my antennae pricked up, as if I recognised something.

We met beside a bonfire, kids running around, burning twigs and sparklers. Belinda was encouraging a waif called Erin to take her three fingers out of her mouth for long enough to light a sparkler. Her own baby was tucked up in a blanket in the house.

When we introduced each other, apparently I said, 'I'm Ervin,' and she said, 'I'm Belinda,' and then I said, 'Belinda – that's a nice name. I know a cow called Belinda.'

She was still living with her daughter's father but one of his friends said that he told everyone she was no good, and that he'd be glad to be rid of her.

So I asked her out and then I asked her to bring her daughter and move in with my sons and me. She said 'Why?' and I said, 'Because you are unhappy.'

She moved in within a month. She said that, in affairs of the heart, she'd never before been sure but, with me, she felt it would work.

We married some years ago. Our three kids witnessed our signatures. We had a barbecue at our oldest son's house and we laughed a lot. It was our twentieth anniversary.

The Kids' Religions

When Dirk was eight he insisted
on hearing *Jesus Christ Superstar*
over and over again as he shuddered
at each and every one
of the thirty-nine lashes.
He even managed to crucify himself
with some rags to the apple tree.
We had to cut him down.
But then he moved on
to torturing his brother instead,
locking him in cupboards
and testing various devices on him.
I don't know how my kids
grew up without claustrophobia;
Miklós did the same thing to Hana.
I'd come in to hear her
humming quietly to herself
from some small dark locked space.

Miklós's religious period started when he was five.
He began to pray.
Once, the older boys had constructed
a ramp to make their toy cars jump
but Miklós's wouldn't jump so he said, 'I'll pray.'
And amid the laughter and derision of the older boys,
he put his fat little hands together, shut his eyes,
frowned hard and mumbled ferociously.
Then he put his car on the ramp and it fairly flew.
That same day we were walking past the wattle tree
and there was a dead blackbird beneath it.

'I'll pray for it,' said Miklós. I thought, 'You poor boy.'
But he kneeled down next to the spreadeagled form
and repeated his fervent actions
and when he opened his eyes, the bird flew away.
'Dad?' said Dirk, his voice quivering.
'You'd better be kind to your brother,' I said.
Miklós stopped praying as quickly as he started.
Perhaps he got disappointed
or maybe just interested in something else.

I think Hana grew out of magical thinking
when the sea wouldn't do what she wanted
or the weather misbehaved.
But, being the youngest, she received good advice
about hanging on to Santa and the tooth fairy.
She says that once she had a vision,
in the toilet, when she was three.
She told us that a blue lady appeared
and said not to tell so many lies.
She was also uncanny with cards.
She was not so much religious, I think,
as intuitive. But I get the feeling
that both she and her mother
find the whole world a miracle.

Little Girls

Little girls are strange and sexy creatures.
They are only about four
when they start practising their wiles
strutting around in pouts
and pretty clothes
and wriggling their garlic bottoms like women.
Luckily
you can distract them easily
or tickle them into writhing heaps of laughter
and they wander off
to play with garden worms
or something.
It's quite shocking
and a relief when they grow out of that stage.
But around thirteen
they do it again
with badly applied make-up
and push-up bras.
They wobble around in ridiculous shoes
and short skirts but this time
it's not aimed at their father.

Shared Brain Cell

Our children say that my wife and I
share a brain cell and it's the only one we've got
because we learned not to make promises
without consulting each other.

They tricked us into pets and lollies and expensive holidays
and goodness knows what else by saying things like:
'If Dad agrees, can we have…' and then,
'Belinda says that, if you agree, we can have…'

Miklós was the master, Hana his apprentice,
and we were left shaking our heads in disbelief,
usually poorer.
Thus we learned to say, 'I'll discuss it with…'

Wishy-washy we looked because wishy-washy
we were, hence the brain cell theory
and, even now, if we happen to say the same thing
at the same time, they say, 'Oh! It fired!'

Pure Luck

Don't you find teenagers great?
I mean, as long as you have no ego left
and can cope with being so stupid.

They try out every possible way
of being trouble, pit themselves
against you and all other grown-ups,

do terrible dangerous things
downright stupid things
and life-enriching things.

And, if they survive,
they're left with a lifetime's memories:
good, sad, embarrassing and funny.

Mine survived. They lost friends to cars
and alcohol but they survived, even though
they walked the same knife edges.

The Practice of Art

What makes an old man
take off all his clothes,
put a rusty bucket on his head,
stand in a field of broken sticks
take a photograph of himself,
and then present the image
above a pile of red sand
in the sterile space of an art gallery?

By which time the piece makes a statement
that is aesthetic as well as political
and the amnesiac viewer gets what it is saying
about our disrespect for the world,

but comments instead about the depth of black
and the shades of white. And it makes
no difference to our degradation of the earth, but
making a difference was never the aim, let's face it.
I can't be worried about the reception of thing.
I am an old man. I have no time to worry
about messages.

What I want my art to do is to carry me
into the heart of creation, the heat of creation,
to the place where my feet
pad softly from crayon to camera
and all I can hear is my own excited heart
because I am about to discover what I do next.

Seeking Sanctuary

I was only eighteen when Australia
opened its wide and friendly arms
to me and I made a home here.
My heart wells with this
red black white yellow earth.
My blood flows with it.
After fifty years even my bones
are made of it, belong to it,
will be buried within it.

I've walked this earth of Australia
minding my own business,
employing people, paying my taxes,
and everyone accepted me
despite my accent.
So it came as a shock recently
when I answered the phone to hear,
'You still around, wog?
Your time is up.'

The hard hot embers of hatred
have been fanned by politicians
like dogs snarling around a bone.
Ordinary people have lost their hearts
so others, like I was, lost people,
who are running from storms
of bullets and cruelty
are incarcerated, frustrated
and treated like dirt.

And all that they are looking for
is safety. They are looking for refuge.
They are refugees.

Who knows what people can bear?

Who knows what people can bear? The blood
that whitened my mother's hair whitened mine also.

And when my dead baby brother returned to her
all grown-up in her addled mind

they put her away and said to me,
'Don't ring. She won't know it's you.'

But two years later she knew enough
to die on my birthday

having asked them to ask me to come.
But they hadn't.

She said, 'He's not coming, is he?'
and pulled the sheet over her head and died.

And me on the other side of the world
unsure what to believe

between the deceits of relatives
wringing their hands for money

money she received from Germany
apparently for her work while a prisoner of war

money that brought my brother back to her
but did not pay for his life.

My Mother

When I was a child, my mother
wasn't there a lot of the time.
And not much wonder
given the grief.
But she didn't protect me.
She didn't care for me
when my stomach growled
and I slept in toilet blocks.

But after she died she came to me.
I said to my wife, 'She's here.'
A sense of her forgiving me
for not being at her deathbed
for not seeing through the lies
of devious relatives.
A forgiveness of sorts,
but can I forgive her?

Lessons in Love

Her mother tried not to look as Hana
went wild and partied, hitch-hiked,
smoked all manner of things,
and loved too many people rather too intimately.

Belinda said, 'Just like me, but earlier.'
She said, 'But this is how they grow,
how they learn to be safe,'
and gave instructions on safe sex and birth control.

Hana, of course, knew it all. Her mother said,
'She could have been run over by a bus
but she's survived this far,'
and she crossed her fingers and covered her eyes.

And Hana has grown into a strong woman,
wise beyond her years. She has a good man
beside her and a baby on her knee.
She is awed and excited by mothering.

Her own well-loved father
died before the baby was born.
She teaches the little one that I am '*Nagy Papa*.'
It is Hungarian for grandfather.

When Hana was a little girl, the society
was so crazy with accusing people of paedophilia
that I was afraid to show her physical affection.
It is wonderful now. She hugs me wholeheartedly

and she and the little one teach me
how to receive love.

The Old-time Communist

A Sri Lankan friend of mine says a culture
is judged on how well it cares for its least fortunate.

A Russian lad on TV the other day said,
'Democracy is like a fight with no rules.'

My mother said, 'Capitalism will gobble itself up.'
My wife says the backs of families are broken.

One friend says TV is to blame; another says God;
another says, 'Gaia will shrug us off, as viruses on her skin.'

Some say famine, some pestilence, some say
that the sun will burn us up.

Meanwhile the Down syndrome boy
plays his tin whistle for pennies.

And in front of Hungry Jack's, in the wind,
an old man plays a toy xylophone long into the night.

He doesn't meet your eyes, even if you
throw some coins into his upturned hat.

It is a sign of age to say 'the good old days'.
I rant and rave. My eyes get beady and angry.

There is not enough money for most and too much for some.
I finger my iPod. I think, 'Even me.'

Belinda's mum said she wished she could come back
to see what happened in fifty years, a hundred.

My son says that, even though they brutalised me,
I am an old-time Communist.

I am not a Communist but someone needs to look after those
who cannot   look after   themselves.

Thanks

There was a woman
who lent me her gloves
when I was eleven and starving.
I was lined up with others to shovel snow,
a bit of work for a bit of food.
But she saw me standing there,
waif that I was, and lent me her gloves.
Such luxury, the warm soft fur.

When I was running in '56,
exhausted, hungry and injured,
there was a man who passed me on the road.
He took me home in his cart, fed me
and put me to bed under huge goose-down covers.
'I can't do much for most,' he said,
'but I can give you a bed.'

There was a couple in Sydney who drove me
halfway across town at five a.m. to catch a train.
They didn't know me; they were just kind.

There was the man with the worry beads,
the doctor and his coat, an old woman
who pointed the way, and many others.

They all disappeared into space and time
with their good hearts because they were strangers.
But I would like to meet each one, and say,

'Thanks.'

Wanting to Make Love to Her

Her full skirt swings with her hips.
Her hair smells of family shampoo and catches sunlight
and I want to make love to her.

Baby at her breast,
she nibbles the small outstretched hand
and I want to make love to her.

Nimble as a doe, she's a wisp of a woman, thin with youth.
My youngest son snuggles into her breasts, inhaling her scent
and I want to make love to her.

She is wearing business clothes and is serious with selling.
Her glasses broken, she peers at a customer, is pale and tired
and I want to make love to her.

She stands naked, smelling of sweat and garden soil.
She snips flowers, arranging them in an ancient green vase
and I want to make love to her.

On the veranda, my oldest boy and she
erupt with laughter and lean a little closer together.
I want to make love to her.

Earrings dangle, catching briefly
on her neck as she bends forward
and I want to make love to her.

Her body finds its mature shape.
She turns, critical, at the mirror
and I want to make love to her.

I am alone with my books
and she is out
but I want to make love to her.

Her step is on the stairs. She is tired and carrying shopping,
her grey hair unkempt around her face
and I want to make love to her.

We lie together, two old people. She twitches in her dream.
My heart is much stronger than my groin
but I want to make love to her.

Magpies

In summer Right Foot sits on the veranda and mimics and sings. He mimics little snippets of other birds: kookaburras, wattlebirds, the small whistles, pops and trills of honeyeaters. He does dog and cat, human-type sounds and in between flutes his magpie melodies.

Right Foot has been the alpha male around here for at least twenty years. When I feed them, the other magpies wait for him to eat first. Then his wife Left Foot eats, and then all of the others. The other birds wait for them even if Right and Left Foot are way down the paddock. They fly in like bombers, straight and low to the ground, lifting just at the last minute to put their gammy feet down. They have all sorts of rituals to trick the crows: acting as decoys while others feed the babies, or hiding meat in the grass for later.

These days Right Foot has a growth on his sore leg; he can hardly put his foot down. He even sits down to eat. I broke my hip a few years ago, osteoporosis apparently. I suppose Right Foot and I are on our way out. Our wives will miss us.

My Friend Death

Just being upright in the world
takes energy and eventually
they lay your body in the earth.

It gives life
to a myriad things
and I am OK with that.

As for what else
might happen
no one knows

but I have experienced
a deep space within myself
a comforting emptiness

my presence within the whole
not separate, not the ego, not I
not limited like that

It feels like silk or syrup
is pure consciousness
absolute freedom.

Within it there is no time
and therefore it was not born
and it will not die.

Bread

Crusty and warm, smelling of yeast
and earth, accompanied by grapes and cheese
and the soft wild herbs under a tree in spring
with the sun building its strength, warming
the soil, warming your winter bones,
sprouting the seeds of grain, holy, holy.

I cut bread as my grandparents did
by holding it against my heart and slicing
the knife in and around. My wife complains
that the end is rough. She slices it on a breadboard
with a serrated knife like a clinician, straight through,
as if it were not a body. Sometimes she even leaves it
the wrong way up. I turn it over patiently.
It is an insult to put the body of Christ on its head.

Old habits die hard, as they say;
I wouldn't call myself a Christian
but a loaf of bread is a loaf of bread
and Jesus was a man in the line
of enlightened teachers. He made
some mistakes and the church many more.
It's ironic that Jesus stood pointing the way
and everyone is still looking at his finger.

He said, 'Cleave the wood
and you'll find me there,
turn a stone and there I'll be,'
or something like that.

Christ in the wood, in the stone,
in the soil that grows the rye,
in the muscles of the baker's hands,
in the sweet yeast smell in the darkest hours,
in the shy girls in aprons counting coins into your hand,
in the sparkling tiles underfoot,
holy, all holy.

And the hand that holds the knife,
the hand of my wife passing a slice,
neat and straight and perfect for toasting.
It sponges with the life of yeast and rye,
with sunshine and the minerals of the earth,
holy, holy, holy, holy.

Awakening

After Ghalib

To whom shall I complain?
What created my life?

A scrap of paper in the hand,
this origami world.

If I had never existed
how could I be sorrowful?

Don't ask of one who limps
the convolutions of the maze.

The frenzy of my desire dances coal-footed
binding me with strips of paper.

Seeking in all places, I find a jewel
that I cannot touch or see.

Like a womb this darkness
that envelops me.

As smooth as honey and as sweet,
it is bottomless and I sink.

Her scent lingers
the oiled skin's memory.

My spine is straight in the hard-backed chair.
A sun glows behind my eyes.

The sky opens to stars.
All of life could be between my thumbs.

The needle and the camel,
crazy people like me slip through.

The dark knot of my heart unravelled.
She bunched it up with her hair.

After discursive dreams, my eyes opened.
Nothing had changed; everything had changed.

I awaken to myself.
It is one of the many ways to die.

Postscript

After Ervin broke his hip at age sixty-eight, he experienced long-term non-specific pain. One specialist told him that it is common for people who have had traumatic childhoods to have such pain.

As a result, Ervin has re-examined his memories. In a painful self-confrontation, he realised that he had seen his stepfather René and his brother René in Hungary after the war, so the memory of their deaths at the hands of the Germans was untrue.

Baby René must have died shortly after the war because Ervin has no later memories of him. He does, however, remember his grandmother telling his mother that he had killed René by putting honey on his dummy. Ervin knew that he hadn't. He assumes René died of natural causes or that his grandmother administered the honey and, either way, blamed him.

He remembers his stepfather leaving Budapest on a bus.

He remembers being told that he had been a brave boy when René and his father had been killed in Germany and assumes the story was rewritten to cover the facts of his brother's death.

At the time of writing this book, it was his hard and fast memory and, given it has been his truth for seventy-three years, the author has left the book unchanged.

www.ingramcontent.com/pod-product-compliance
Lightning Source LLC
Chambersburg PA
CBHW070915080526
44589CB00013B/1304